HENRY EDWARDS HUNTINGTON

A Brief Biography

by James Thorpe

The Huntington Library • San Marino, California

Cover Illustrations:
View from the mansion, north toward the mountains
Henry Edwards Huntington, circa 1920

Title Page Illustration:
Cartoon from *Los Angeles Daily Times,* January 21, 1908

ISBN 0–87328–160–8

Printed by Publishers Press, Salt Lake City, Utah
Designed by Karen Harms

The Huntington
1151 Oxford Road, San Marino, California 91108

1850–1869

is parents named him Henry Edwards Huntington* when he was born, on February 27, 1850, in the small town of Oneonta in the Susquehanna Valley of central New York state. The name Edwards was in honor of his maternal grandmother's family. She had been Sally Edwards, a descendant of the eminent religious philosopher Jonathan Edwards, whose memory was kept alive in the family through the continued use of his last name. The Huntington family also had several notable members of whom Edward was a direct descendant, including members of the Continental Congress, generals in the American Revolution, and (in Samuel Huntington) a signer of the Declaration of Independence and president of the Continental Congress. Edward was interested in these matters and in everything that involved his family, especially his immediate family.

Despite this impressive background, his family was in modest financial circumstances. After his parents married in 1840, they bought a house and farm in Oneonta, and his father opened a general store to supply the needs of this farming community of some two thousand persons. The Huntingtons had seven children, Edward being the middle one. When he was less than a year old, his mother wrote to her sister about how skillfully "little Eddy" was able to push a wagon back and forth on the kitchen floor with an older brother in it.

Edward and the other children had plenty of activities in Oneonta as they grew older. In the summer they gathered wild strawberries, swam, fished, played ball or croquet, flew kites, and had bonfires. In the autumn they looked for chestnuts and made

* *When H. E. Huntington was a child, he was called "Eddy" by his family and "Ed" by his friends. When he was older, the name "Edwards" was used for him on formal occasions, and "Edward" by his family and by everyone who knew him well.*

Above: Huntington's parents, Solon and Harriet, in their early married years.
Below: The Huntington family house in Oneonta.

jack-o-lanterns; in the winter they went skating and sliding and chose teams for snow-balling. Indoors they played hide and seek in the family barn and jumped onto the hay from the rafters. In the spring they searched for wildflowers and explored the crevices in the rocky hills.

Special days had special pleasures. The public exhibition and drill of the volunteer fire department (all neighbors and friends, dressed up in their bright uniforms) brought everybody out, as did the drilling of the two regiments of state militia on the river flats by the village. The Fourth of July began with a cannon salute at sunrise and ended (after a day of music and speeches) with an elaborate fireworks display near the Huntington house. But the greatest excitement occurred on the day of the circus, with an extravaganza in and around its canvas city. It was on circus day that Edward had his first experience as an entrepreneur, when he was eight or nine. He built a covered booth where he could sell candy, peanuts, lemonade, and cider (for five cents a glass). At the end of the long day he had cleared, he said later, "what looked bigger than anything I ever since have made—eight dollars and fifty-five cents!"

The Huntington house was well supplied with books, and reading was a special pleasure for Edward and for the rest of the family. The two grandmothers visited often and enthralled the children with their stories of the old days. There was a good deal of music in the house, with a piano and a violin, and the family all regularly attended the Presbyterian church and the children went to its church school.

But there were also chores to do. Edward and his brothers had to keep the wood box in the kitchen full, and they had to take the cows to pasture in the morning and bring them back in the evening. And there was school. Edward went to the public school, which had about seventy-five pupils. Edward was a conscientious student. When he was twelve, he wrote to his older sister about his work on grammar. "I intend to go through my grammar tomorrow and then commence it again next day, for I intend to go through it

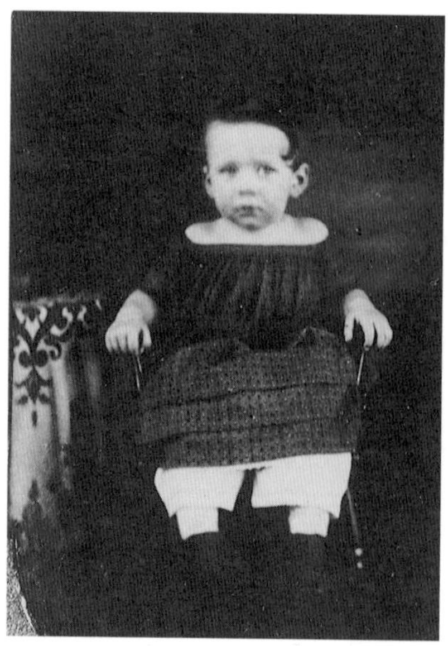

Huntington under the age of two (*left*) and at age eight (*right*).

again and again. For I want to learn to talk correctly, as I have not learned yet."

He learned about death early. Before he was ten, three of his six siblings had died—both of his older brothers and one of his younger sisters. These deaths drew the family closer together and doubtless contributed to Edward's feeling of the centrality of family to human experience.

When Edward was twelve, he went alone by stagecoach to visit his maternal grandparents over a hundred miles away. Two days later he wrote to his mother as directed. His letter reveals a good deal about what kind of person he was at that time.

Dear Mother

You know that you told me to write the next day after I got here. But Uncle Darwin said that he would write so that you would know that I got here safe and sound, and he said that I could write today. Well, I will not talk about writing. Now I would like to know how you all are, and how you get along with your work. Uncle Charles has come here and while he has gone up to Aunt Marcia's I am writing to you, and Leonora and Will and Carrie. Does she walk, and has she got the measles? Why don't you write? (Say hey!—are you bashful?) Come, write and tell me how you are, and all of you. I had a pleasant ride of 8 miles on the lake, and I got here just in time, for that was the last time that they were going. You told me I need not write a very long letter at first. So, good morning!

HEH

PS Write soon

1869–1872

Edward finished school in Oneonta when he was seventeen and went to work right away as a clerk in the local hardware store. He continued in this job for two years while living at home. Then at age nineteen he told his mother, "I am getting to that age that I do not like to feel dependent on anyone." So he moved about a hundred miles away to the town of Cohoes, New York (near Albany), where he got a job in the hardware store run by the husband of his older sister. But this work did not prove very promising, and after four months he moved on to the greater challenge of New York City. There in 1870 (at the age of twenty) he was able to get only a menial job as a porter in a wholesale hardware company, but he was soon promoted to order clerk. He lived in a boarding house in Brooklyn and worked very hard to learn the business.

He spent nearly every Sunday at the house of his father's younger brother, Collis P. Huntington, who (with his wife Elizabeth Stoddard) was now living comfortably at 65 Park Avenue. After twenty years of hard work and struggle in building the railroad to California, Collis was rich and influential and well disposed toward his relatives. His house was a gathering place, especially on Sundays and holidays, and out-of-town relatives were regularly invited to come to New York for visits. Edward's mother and his siblings were there several times a year, as were Elizabeth's relatives, including Mary Alice Prentice (Elizabeth's niece and the sister of Elizabeth and Collis's adopted daughter,

Clara) from Sacramento. She was two years younger than Edward, and they became friends and corresponded regularly.

Edward was lonely in New York, and he greatly enjoyed the visits to his uncle's house. He went with Collis and Elizabeth every Sunday to Henry Ward Beecher's church, enjoyed the sermons, and also attended the Sunday school. On Sunday afternoons, Collis would often take him for a carriage ride in Central Park. He wrote his mother that "I always have such a pleasant time up there. Uncle and Aunt are both very kind to me; and if anyone appreciates it, I think that I do. I feel so thankful tonight to feel that I have so many friends, the more so because I do not feel that I am so deserving of them." He missed home and family, and he said, "I tell you a boy knows how to appreciate Father & Mother when he gets away from home."

Edward felt that there was no future for him in the hardware store in New York if he wanted "to amount to something." After a year there, Collis offered him the job of running a sawmill he owned in West Virginia. Edward jumped at the chance, and in April 1871 (at the age of twenty-one) he took over the mill. His job was to oversee the production of railroad ties from trees cut in the area. He had a foreman and some thirty men, working two shifts. His job was to insure a supply of logs, to manage the operation of the mill, and to arrange for the disposition of the ties. He worked very hard, sometimes through the night, in trying to save his logs when the river flooded. Collis sent him frequent letters of advice and commentary on the operations, particularly urging careful accounting and frugality: "see that not a dollar is wasted that can possibly be saved." Edward slept in his office at the mill and had his meals at the home of the local Presbyterian minister. He came to know the area—it was his first time out of New York state—and the people ("rebels" he called them), whom he found hospitable and cordial, though he thought the women did not know how to cook properly, always serving fried foods and coffee. His correspondence with Mary increased, and he saw her regularly on his visits to Collis in New York. In April 1872 (when he was twenty-two and she was twenty) he wrote to his mother that they were engaged to be married.

1872–1881

ollis had become restless with his ownership of the sawmill and in the spring of 1872 began saying that he wanted to sell it. General Richard Franchot, formerly Collis's chief lobbyist in Washington, agreed to buy it for his son S. P. Franchot, who had just graduated from Union College, and Collis arranged for Edward to own a half interest in the mill through a loan. Young Franchot came to board at the minister's house, and in the spring of 1873 the two inexperienced young men went to work in a partnership financed by their elders.

Problems arose immediately. Some of their shipments of lumber were rejected, sales were very slow, buyers did not pay promptly, and the financial panic of 1873 limited their access to capital.

In the midst of these troubles, Edward and Mary were married in November 1873 at the home of her aunt in Newark, New Jersey. They rented a house in West Virginia and set up housekeeping. Franchot objected strenuously to Edward spending money that the firm badly needed on furnishings. Edward opened a general store on the side; beside displeasing both Franchot and Collis, this effort brought in no revenue.

In June 1874, after a trial of about a year, the two young men decided to break up their partnership, to the shock and horror of their elders. Their lack of both experience and capital worked against them in a business that was marginal at best, and virtually impossible under the economic conditions of the time. Edward wrote his mother that "I do not think that Uncle Collis has done what he could for my interest," but he assured her that he was not discouraged: "Thank the Lord I have got a little spunk in my disposition."

As part of the settlement between the two partners, Edward had to give his library to Franchot. This collection—a great book collector's first library—had cost him $1,700 and numbered more than a hundred volumes. These books, bought to be read and kept, were mainly sets of the works of recent writers (like Ruskin, Whittier, Lowell, Dickens, and Scott) and historical compilations

Mary Alice Prentice and Huntington at about the time of their wedding in 1873.

concerning American and ancient history; but it also had a few unusual items, like nine volumes of Isaac Disraeli's literary and historical anecdotes.

The sawmill was returned to Collis, who gave Edward the job of looking after the properties (after shutting down the mill) for a salary of $50 a month. Edward agreed, but in the meantime he tried (unsuccessfully) to raise money to open a general store. He kept asking whether Collis had any other job he might fill, but Collis said he did not. Early in 1876 the young Huntingtons' first child was born, a boy they named Howard Edwards for Edward's dead brother and for Edward's uncle Howard Saunders. Soon thereafter, Edward's father offered him the job of managing his farms and other properties in and around Oneonta, at a salary of $75 a month. When Collis could offer no alternative, he accepted.

Edward and Mary spent five years in Oneonta at the family home. Mary managed the household, as Edward's mother was away visiting relatives much of the time. Edward saw to the renting of his father's farms and houses (which were numerous but of little value), collected the rents, paid the taxes, took care of repairs and maintenance, and kept the accounts. Soon after they got settled, Collis turned over the management of his Oneonta houses and farms to Edward in place of his younger brother Willard, whom he called to New York and soon sent to California.

Edward and Mary had two more children, Clara and Elizabeth, in Oneonta. Their family flourished, and Mary was absorbed in the welfare of the three children. Her other interests were clothes and social activities. Edward's interest was in work, but his career was at a standstill. In 1881, at the age of thirty-one, he had tried several different lines of work and had not been successful in any of them. He was delighted when Collis asked him if he would like to go to the South and assume responsibility for laying a railroad line in Kentucky and Tennessee.

1881–1892

Edward spent the next eleven years learning the railroad business from the ground up. During the first year, he was responsible for laying one hundred twenty-five miles of track in western Kentucky and western Tennessee, with a work crew including a foreman and twenty-four men. Then he supervised the grading and building of the railroad shops in Kentucky; he acted as purchasing agent, and he made studies of the railroad properties that were in trouble. In 1885 Collis made him division superintendent of the Kentucky Central Railroad, despite his lack of operating experience. Edward's first major job, in addition to running the railroad, was to build a mile-long bridge across the Ohio River between Covington and Cincinnati so that the railroad could increase its revenue with Ohio terminals. In the meantime, Collis decided to have the railroad declared bankrupt and Edward was appointed receiver by the court to continue to run the railroad. In due course, it was bought by a group acting for Collis, and Edward continued to run it. Finally, in 1891, Collis sold it to the L & N Railroad at a good profit, and Edward's railroading career in Tennessee and Kentucky was over.

During these years his experience broadened and deepened. He learned how to look at property and appraise its future potential, to size up and deal effectively with fellow workers at all levels, and to analyze financial reports to discover the strengths and weaknesses of a company. He also began to learn how to make money grow. Although his salary was never more than $350 a month during these years, at the end of this time his net worth was over $600,000. He ran a commissary for employees, he bought and sold securities in various companies he knew well, and he acquired land in Kentucky and Texas. And he began to build another library for himself. By 1886, he had accumulated about 2,000 volumes at a cost of some $5,000. It was an excellent assortment of recent nineteenth-century writers, with a good many earlier and foreign writers; the books were not rare or collector's items, but books to read, to own, and to cherish.

These were difficult years for the members of Edward's immediate family. They were all together only about half of the time. Often moving around, they stayed in boarding houses or temporary rentals in Louisville, Covington, and Cincinnati. Mary and the children were sometimes in Sacramento (for as much as six months at a time) and sometimes in Oneonta. Most of them had

A family gathering in Oneonta by the side of the Huntington residence, c. 1900. Huntington is standing among their four children. His mother (with a scarf over her head) and his wife are seated on the bench in front, with three other relatives present.

recurrent illnesses, including two long spells of malaria from which Edward suffered. In 1883 they had their fourth (and last) child, Marian, after an unexpected and unwanted pregnancy. Collis's wife Elizabeth died of cancer, and the next year he married Arabella Worsham (called Belle), whom he had known for twenty years. And in 1890, after fifteen years of inactivity, Edward's father died. Edward handled the estate (of about $25,000) and thereafter provided the extra money that his mother needed for her support.

Edward had proved himself, by hard work and intelligence, to be a good railroad manager. But when the L & N took over the Kentucky Central, there was nothing left there for him to manage. Collis's major holdings were in California, and in 1892 he invited Edward to go to San Francisco as first assistant to the president of the Southern Pacific Company. Since the president (Collis) was rarely in San Francisco, Edward found himself as the central figure in the operation of the largest and most important business in the state of California.

1892–1900

dward made his first trip to California in April 1892 in the company of Collis and Belle and their entourage. They went by way of Los Angeles and spent the night with J. De Barth Shorb at his San Marino Ranch in the San Gabriel Valley, among orange groves and with mountains and hills looming up in the distance. Edward was entranced by the beauty of the setting. "I thought then," he said later, "that it was the prettiest place I had ever seen.

When he arrived in San Francisco, it would be hard to imagine a more difficult situation than the one he came into as assistant to the president of the Southern Pacific. Collis had recently managed to depose Leland Stanford from the presidency and had gained Stanford's undying enmity by suggesting that he had used the company for personal and political gain. The four owners (the interests of Huntington, Stanford, Hopkins, and Crocker) were hostile to one another, and the alignments and antagonisms spread throughout the staff. The company was the object of intense admiration and violent hatred in the press and throughout the state. In addition, Edward had to manage through the financial panic of 1893, when banks were closing everywhere and when there was often not enough money to pay wages or bills on time, and through the national railway strike of 1894, which created havoc in California. He was successful in helping the railroad get through these difficult times in the 1890s, but his public reputation was mixed. In some quarters he was praised for his organizational ability, for getting good results from his subordinates and creating a friendlier atmosphere. He himself was proudest of increasing the profitability of the company. In other quarters, however, he was bitterly denounced as a person greedy for power and in charge of the SP's "Bureau for the Creation of Enemies." Still, on the whole, he was a moderately popular figure.

Edward and his family lived in a hotel for a year after they moved to San Francisco, but then they bought a new three-story house (for $50,000) and began an active life. They joined a country club, began to invite guests, and rented a pew in the First Presbyterian Church. The children took music, language, and riding lessons. The Huntingtons' son Howard went to Harvard for an engineering education, and Edward's mother began to come from Oneonta to spend the winters with them. They took various short family trips together—to Monterey, Los Angeles, Riverside, and to a

H. E. and C. P. Huntington on a street in San Francisco in the 1890s.

summer house they rented in northern California. Mary took their oldest daughter to Europe for a two-month trip, while the younger ones stayed in Oneonta. Each of them had occasional bouts of illness but Edward was the one most prone to have "hard colds" or some other malady that kept him at home for a week or two at a time.

In San Francisco in the 1890s he devoted a good deal of his time to visiting book shops. He extended his collection by adding such writers as Thoreau, Hawthorne, Sterne, and Swift. In addition, he acquired historical writers like Bancroft and Parkman, as well as foreign and classical authors, and many specialty items like Gelett Burgess and Jeremy Taylor. In addition, he began to buy art—pictures for their residence, watercolors and jades, and basic books about British, American, and French art.

Edward was very busy with his work, as usual. In addition to his responsibilities in San Francisco, he traveled frequently all over California, inspecting the lines, considering where extensions would be financially most advantageous, and meeting groups of the leading businessmen in most of the larger towns and cities in the state. He was especially drawn to the climate and beauty of the Los Angeles area, and it was said that "this portion of the land has no more ardent supporter, and no one with more confidence in its future than young Mr. Huntington." He had been responsible for the street railway system in San Francisco for several years, and in 1898 he formed a syndicate, with himself as the majority contributor to take over and consolidate the ailing street railway companies in Los Angeles.

Edward was anxious to be made a vice president of the Southern Pacific, and though several opportunities came up during these years, he was passed over to placate the other major owners. At last, in 1899, Collis arranged for his investment bankers to buy out the Crocker and Stanford interests, and Edward was rewarded by being made second vice president, and then first vice president. But his tenure did not last long. Collis died in 1900, and the investment bankers put their own men into all of the top jobs. Edward was sorely disappointed, as he had yearned to succeed Collis as president.

Instead, he was out of a job. And in the loss of Collis, he was without his mentor, his surrogate father, and his principal employer for almost thirty years. He wrote to his mother that "no one can ever fill his place in my heart. Oh, Mother, you can never know what he was to me. So kind, so good, and with such a true heart."

There was some consolation for Edward in the bequests left him by Collis. He received one-third of Collis's Southern Pacific stock and a part of the residue of the estate, in all about $12 to $15 million. (The whole estate was worth about $50 million, and there were bequests and trusts for many family members. Belle received by far the largest share, about $20 to $25 million plus ownership of all of his art and real estate for her lifetime.) Edward's annual salary had gone up from $10,000 to $27,000 in the course of these years, and by canny investing, his net worth had increased to $1 million. Now with his uncle's bequest, he was seen as a "Really Rich Man" with "a colossal fortune." His poise had carried him through his earlier failures; it now had to carry him through the sudden public fame his wealth had brought him.

1900–1910

ven though he was out of a regular job, Edward remained a hard worker. He was drawn to Southern California to manage and develop his street railway system. At first he stayed at the Van Nuys Hotel, but soon took an apartment in the Jonathan Club. He was often needed in New York by the lawyers for Collis's estate—especially since Belle was mostly in Europe with her son Archer and his wife Helen—and he had a regular office there and a suite of rooms at the Metropolitan Club. He knew the details of Collis's business and he spent regular periods in New York helping with the settlement of the estate.

Mary spent much of her time travelling. Beginning in 1901, she took their daughters to Europe frequently and passed the summers in their vacation home in Northern California. When

The four Huntington children as young adults in San Francisco.
Clockwise from upper left: Howard, c. 1900; Clara, Elizabeth, and Marian, c. 1910.

Howard finished his studies at Harvard in 1902, he was given a management job in the street railway company in Los Angeles and moved into his father's suite at the Jonathan Club.

For the first ten years after Collis's death, Edward's main business activity was in Southern California. His feeling for the area had been love at first sight. "You come here," he wrote later, "and you are conquered. When I first went to California, I traveled east, north, and south from one end of the state to the other, even going off the beaten paths by team and studying every section carefully. I came to the conclusion then that the greatest natural advantages, those of climate as well as every other condition, lay in Southern California and that is why I made it the field of my endeavor."

His endeavor included greatly extending the electric street railway lines, while developing land and providing utilities for the expanding population of Southern California. His lines became a network that connected the central city, the outlying towns, and the beaches in a high-speed (fifty to sixty miles per hour) and inexpensive (five cents within the city) transit system. The expansion moved at a remarkable pace; less than a hundred miles of lines in 1900 became almost a thousand by 1910. Or, as the newspapers put it, "Count that day lost which ere the setting sun / Sees not a beach resort or trolley line begun." By 1910 his street railway system was widely regarded (even by the members of the American Street Railway Association) as the best one in the world.

Edward also acquired large quantities of land all over the county. He bought sixteen substantial parcels in downtown Los Angeles and about 11,000 acres outside of the central city in nearly every direction. Most of his suburban property was subdivided into half-acre lots for sale at $300 to $500 each, with the average cost of building a house on these lots about $2,000. He was keenly interested in making it possible for people to have their own homes on their own land and still be able to get to and from their places of work quickly and inexpensively. He also organized a series of companies to provide electricity, gas, and water to the people of Southern California at a time before municipalities were doing so.

He made a good deal of money from these activities, but he never tried to maximize his profits. He was a lover of Southern California before he was a businessman. "I could have made a whole lot more money out of this country than I have done," he said, "if money-making had not been tempered with real affection for this region."

It was a period of prosperity and growth in Southern California. Between 1900 and 1910, the population of the City of Los Angeles rose from 100,000 to 300,000, the official figures for property values of Los Angeles County rose 428 percent, and the other economic indicators all evidenced a bright present and a brighter future. Edward was usually given the credit for it all, in a very personal way. The street railways were known as "Mr. Huntington's lines," the Pacific Electric Building (the largest building west of Chicago) was "the Huntington Building," and all extensions and improvements were attributed to "Mr. Huntington."

People felt that Edward was mainly responsible for all the good things that had happened to Southern California, and he began to be treated like a hero, almost as a mythical figure. Honors were heaped upon him, in the form of dinners and testimonials and chairmanships. A more light-hearted tribute was a popular anecdote that joined Huntington and God together. In the version told to the Los Angeles City Council in 1906 (as a "true story"), a father was taking his six-year-old daughter out for a trolley tide. "Papa, who owns all these cars?" asked the daughter. "Mr. Huntington," the father replied. Later that day, while sitting by the ocean, the daughter asked again, "What place is this, Papa?" "Huntington Beach," the father promptly stated. "Who owns it?" "Mr. Huntington," the father replied. Later, the child asked, "Who owns the ocean, Papa?" "God," he replied. After a moment of pondering, the child asked, "But Papa, how did he get it away from Mr. Huntington?"

Edward was in San Francisco very little during these years. The three older children got married and established homes of their own. Edward was always generous with the children on birthdays and Christmas, as well as for trips and allowances. At the time of their marriages, they each received a $250,000 trust fund and a new house of their choice. In 1906, Mary filed for divorce on the grounds that Edward had deserted her. He did not contest the divorce; in the settlement, she received the San Francisco house and about $2.5 million. Their marriage had been unhappy because of their incompatibility (with Edward mainly interested in work and Mary absorbed in raising the children and in social activities). "We have been very unhappy for years," he wrote to a daughter, "and getting more so as the years went by. No one can ever know how much I have suffered." He concluded by saying, "How very dear my children are to me, and how much I regret that I have not been able to make your lives happier. I can only say I have done my best. With a heart full of love for my dear child. . .".

Edward did find time to devote his attention increasingly to gardening and book and art collecting. In 1903 he bought the Shorb Ranch of five hundred acres (with the house in which he had spent his first night in California) and three hundred additional contiguous acres. He began to spend Sundays and holidays walking around the ranch, enjoying its natural beauty, and thinking about the improvements he wanted to make. Sometimes he spent the night with his next door neighbors, the George Pattons, so that he could have a good walk on the grounds before breakfast. He tramped all over the place, laying out paths and roads. Gradually he began to develop the central part of the ranch with lily ponds, a cactus garden, palms, flowering trees, and shrubs. He saved the seeds of avocados from the Jonathan Club to start an avocado grove. He was also thinking about a residence from which to enjoy all this natural beauty. He decided to tear down the old Shorb house and replace it with a large two-story structure with a spacious attic and a full basement. He made sketches of what he wanted and hired Myron Hunt as his architect. The plan struck Hunt at first like "a library with a few rooms about it." After some modifications, construction proceeded, with Edward in almost daily attendance, talking with the workmen and enjoying the building

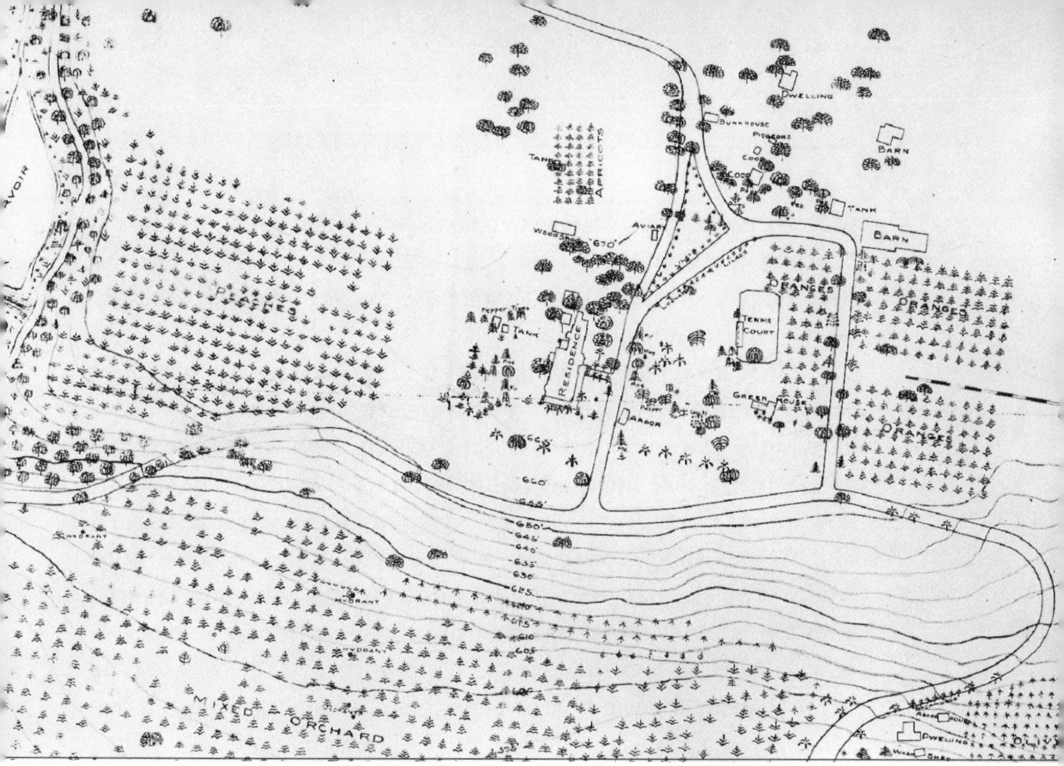

Above: Drawing of the central part of the Shorb Ranch shortly after Huntington bought it in 1903.

Below: Huntington on the porch of the neighboring Patton house in 1903, between Mr. and Mrs. George S. Patton. On the left, standing, is George S. Patton, Jr. (later a general) and seated is Patton's sister Susan; on the right is Hancock Banning.

process. Hunt said, "No owner ever had half so much joy in the building of a house as Henry E. Huntington has found." The job was completed in 1910, and the house was the centerpiece of the increasingly beautiful ranch.

Edward's interest in books and art underwent a radical change during these years. He developed from a modest collector of material of general interest to a relatively sophisticated collector of rare material of international importance. He began to do business with the best dealers in New York and Philadelphia, he learned much more about collecting, and he bought several libraries of books as well as many rare individual items. His collection came to have a modest renown. But first and foremost he was a reader of books. After he had spent the Christmas of 1907 by himself, he wrote to a daughter that "Christmas has come and gone and it was a happy one for me even if I had my turkey all by my lonely. I wish I had been with my children, but as I could not be I made the best of it and really spent a very pleasant evening surrounded by my old friends (my Books) which give me so much pleasure, and I am never at a loss to know what to do with myself."

His art acquisitions were greatly encouraged by the challenge of his new house, which was often described by others as "a Palace." His first major art purchase, for the walls of his library room, was five Beauvais tapestries (from designs by Boucher), previously owned by Louis XV, for $577,000. What was of first importance to him was that he liked them. To a friend he wrote, "I don't want you to miss seeing five tapestries I have at my new home. I have never seen anything that I like quite so well." He also bought a good deal of French furniture, some silk carpets, and several paintings by Romney, Lawrence, Raeburn, and Reynolds. Always it had to be something he really liked.

He was having more and more "enjoyment and fun" from these interests, and in 1908 he said that he was planning to retire from the active personal management of his businesses. He did so at the end of 1910, when his net assets totaled $55 million. He turned over the management of his Pacific Electric Railway, his

Huntington Land and Improvement Company, and his various other enterprises to his trusted colleagues.

1911–1914

In spite of his plans to retire, Edward found himself busier than ever, and his interest in the ranch kept growing. New developments between 1911 and 1914 included the conversion of a tangled canyon into a complete Japanese garden and the acquisition of a large number of rare, primitive plants known as cycads.

He made some important strides as a collector. The real turning points in his career, both as a book and art collector, took place in 1911. In April he acquired (for $1.25 million) the famous E. Dwight Church library. It contained a wonderful collection of very rare and unique material (such as the manuscript of Franklin's *Autobiography,* 22 incunabula, 12 Shakespeare folios, 37 Shakespeare quartos, and 1,500 choice early Americana items). Two weeks later the auction sale of the Robert Hoe library began. Hoe's library was generally considered the finest private collection in the

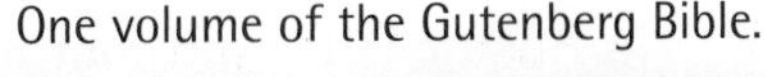

One volume of the Gutenberg Bible.

United States, and its sale was hailed in London and New York as "the greatest event of its kind in the annals of book auctions." The star attraction, offered on the first evening, was the first substantial book printed from movable type, the Gutenberg Bible, on vellum, in two volumes. After spirited bidding, Edward bought it for $50,000, twice the amount ever before paid for a book. The news of this purchase swept the country. One friend teased him by writing, "I have known for many years that you were sadly in need of the influence imparted by the constant use of Holy Writ, but I did not suppose you would feel the need of $50,000 worth of it 'in a bunch'." Edward paid him back by replying that he was chagrined to learn that he "could buy one for ten cents, the contents of which would probably have done me as much good as the one I have." Edward dominated all other sessions of the sale and ended by buying (for about $1 million) everything he wanted, about half of the whole library. He was widely described as having "leaped into fame as a book collector" with what was expected to be "the largest and most valuable private library in this country."

It was also in 1911 that Edward entered the big time as an art collector. He had been buying paintings for a dozen years and had about fifty pictures, mostly of modest quality and interest. But in August 1911, just four months after his big book acquisitions, he bought three stellar paintings by Thomas Gainsborough (*Edward–2d Viscount Ligonier, Penelope–Viscountess Ligonier,* and *Juliana Lady Petre*) from Joseph Duveen for $775,000. These were truly major works of art, and they set the direction of the painting collection toward major English works of the Georgian period and established a level of very high quality. Edward, who was in New York, did not make this purchase until he had gotten Belle, who was in Europe, to look at the paintings and give him her opinion of them.

There had been frequent rumors from 1906 onward that Edward and Belle were planning to be married. Each vehemently denied these rumors. By 1912, Howard's wife wrote one of her sisters-in-law that Edward was "madly in love" with Belle and "does nothing but talk about her," that they spent much of the time together in New York, and that they were planning to be married, despite the fact that Belle was still in mourning for Collis. They were indeed married in July 1913 in Paris. She had gone to Europe before him, and they met in Paris. He had not told anyone in advance of their plan to be married, and his children were surprised by the news. Edward wrote to his sister: "I cannot tell you how happy I am, my dear Sister, and I hope to make up for all I have lost and again have a home, and a home such as I never had. Belle is so good and kind to me, and I know she will make my life a happy one." When Edward wrote her again, a few days later, he said, "I can never tell you how very happy I am. Belle is so sweet. Good and kind, wishing me to have the best of everything. Which is something so entirely new to me. I am very sure, my dear Sister, I am going to be very happy in our new life. In fact, I feel that I am just beginning to live." After a short automobile trip to southern France and Switzerland, they returned to Paris and Edward leased the Chateau Beauregard, an estate near Versailles, as a place for them to stay on future trips to Europe.

Arabella as a young woman (*left*) and in the 1890s in San Francisco (*right*).

Their wedding was treated as very important news in the newspapers, which communicated the full details to the public. The main themes were the marriage of a rich widow to her late husband's nephew ("Bride Is An Aunt of Husband") and the alleged reuniting of a large fortune. (This second theme was entirely untrue, as Belle kept her art, property, money, and other belongings intact for her own use. She was generous in her benefactions in memory of Collis, and at her death, her entire estate was inherited by her son Archer. None of it went to the benefit of Edward or his collections or his children.) The marriage created some family tensions. Edward's daughters thought the marriage "very, very repulsive" and did not feel friendly toward their father or Belle for at least five years, well after the death of their mother in 1916.

Belle was a couple of years younger than Edward. She had been unusually attractive when she was young, and in 1901 one of Edward's daughters wrote him that she "never saw anyone with so much magnetism." And the same daughter wrote to her fiancé that Belle was "very responsive and a very cultivated woman. She is so sweet. She is very romantic herself, though she certainly wouldn't give one that impression at a glance; she has such excellent taste. She is a dear. Know you will like her. And bright." Some people, on the other hand, were offended by what they considered her haughty and aloof manner. Her poor vision may have contributed to this view of her. By the time she was in her thirties, her sight was seriously impaired; later she could see objects only at close range and with the help of thick glasses, and she needed a companion to hold her arm while walking and to read to her. She became obese in her forties; even after losing forty-five pounds one winter, she was still heavy, with broad shoulders, wide lips and prominent lower cheeks. But to Edward she was always a person of charm.

She was born in Richmond, Virginia. Her father died when she was about seven, and her mother supported the family by running a boarding house. Her two brothers both worked for Collis in responsible positions, one of them (like Edward) serving as a division superintendent on one of Collis's railroads. She and Collis were married in 1884, a year after his wife Elizabeth had died and when her son Archer, to whom she was deeply devoted, was fourteen. (The identity of Archer's father is uncertain—probably either Collis or John Worsham to whom she was said to have been married at an early age.) By 1884 she had already accumulated considerable means through astute dealing in securities and in New York real estate. She and Collis lived a lavish life at their several residences and in Europe. After Collis's death in 1900, Belle turned seriously to art collecting; she acquired many splendid paintings, and by 1910 she had become a major force in the world of art.

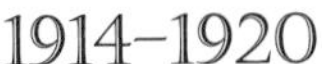

1914–1920

After Edward and Belle returned to New York in the autumn of 1913, he gave up his apartment at the Metropolitan Club and moved into her house at 2 East 57th Street. They made their first visit to Southern California together in January 1914, and this was the first time that the new residence on the ranch had ever been occupied. Upon arrival they drove all around the grounds, and then Edward took great pleasure in showing Belle the entire house, room by room by room. They had a quiet, agreeable visit of three months, with very few social engagements beyond those with family and some of Edward's closest friends. When Belle heard that Archer and his wife Helen were about to leave for Europe, they hurried back to New York so that Belle could see Archer before he left.

Within a month Edward and Belle also set out from New York for France to take up residence in the Chateau Beauregard, which had been thoroughly renovated in accordance with Edward's detailed directions (and at a cost of $100,000). Soon after their arrival, the turmoil preceding the outbreak of the World War began. Nevertheless, they set out on an automobile trip to Germany; near the border they were urged to turn back and reluctantly agreed. The next day war was declared. Archer and Helen were detained in Germany because he was mistaken for a Russian grand duke; Edward frantically cabled his friends to get the American authorities (the secretary of state, President Wilson's secretary, and various ministers) to effect their release, and the diplomatic pressure worked. When the French army took over the grounds of the Chateau Beauregard (including the horses, cattle, and automobiles), Edward was ready to leave for home, but Belle preferred to stay in France, "declaring that she did not think there was any danger." When Archer and Helen got to London, he began to urge his mother to leave, and at last sent an emissary with insistent messages to her. Finally she agreed, the agent picked up her jewelry and valuables from the bank, and her thirty-five trunks were duly packed. Duveen, the art dealer, borrowed an automobile from the British Embassy, drove Henry and Belle to the port, and arranged for berths and exit visas for them to go to England. In London, they were reunited with Archer and Helen and soon made reservations to return to New York. On the evening before their departure, Edward went to an auction and was able to get a book he especially wanted, a first edition of Bunyan's *Pilgrim's Progress.*

Back in New York, Edward got to work on his library. For the first time his collection of books and manuscripts had ample room. Instead of being stacked on chairs and tables and the floor—with the need to move books to provide space for a guest to sit down—his library now came to occupy a whole floor of the house. He had his books all around him, and he spent his time reading and sorting and, with the help of his secretary, cataloging his collection. Early in 1915 it became evident that he needed professional assistance, and he hired as his librarian George Watson Cole (who had earlier compiled the seven-volume catalog of the Church library) and half a dozen young librarians as catalogers. They were confronted by unsorted piles of thousands and thousands of rare books and manuscripts, and acquisitions were pouring in faster than they could sort the earlier ones. Between 1913 and 1920, Edward bought twenty-four large collections of books and manuscripts and thousands of individual items from dealers all over the

United States and Europe. For one example, in 1917 he bought (for $1 million) the Bridgewater House library (of 4,400 volumes and 12,000 manuscripts), a family collection begun in Queen Elizabeth's reign and continued by the Earls of Ellesmere and Dukes of Bridgewater. It contained, for example, the Ellesmere manuscript of Chaucer's *Canterbury Tales* and 2,500 manuscript plays of the eighteenth and early nineteenth centuries.

The fame of Edward's library spread rapidly in the academic world, and by 1915 many scholars were seeking permission to use his rare books and manuscripts. Edward gladly agreed, and when the numbers increased, he set aside a large table next to his own desk for their use. People came from Yale, Columbia, Harvard, Wellesley,

Agreement to purchase the Bridgewater Library for $1 million.

H. E. HUNTINGTON
THE BROAD-EXCHANGE
NEW YORK

February 27,1917.

Messrs Sotheby Wilkinson & Hodge

Dear Sirs

I hereby confirm the purchase by me of the Library,known as the "Bridgewater Library" of the Right Hon. The Earl of Ellesmere,London,as described in the printed Catalogue and check list of said Library for the sum of one million dollars ($1,000,000.00) in United States Coin or its equivalent,payable as follows:

Upon delivery of the first one half of said library, the sum of $250,000.00 in cash and a promissory note for the sum of $250,000.00 payable in two (2) months from said date of delivery. The balance of said purchase price, $500,000.00 to be paid upon delivery of the second one half of said Library in two (2) notes of $250,000.00 each,payable respectively in four and six months from the date of delivery of the first half of said Library. Delivery of Books to be made at the Lincoln Safe Deposit Company,42nd Street, New York City and a receipt given subject to treir proving correct according to check lists.

All risks of insurance are to be assumed by me from the time of delivery of said books at the Lincoln Safe Deposit Company.

It is understood and agreed that a reasonable time will be allowed to check the collection with catalogue and check lists.

It is further understood and agreed that if a portion of said library is lost in transportation,the price to be paid is to be reduced proportionately for the remainder.

H E Huntington

Accepted. Sotheby Wilkinson & Hodge

Princeton, Pennsylvania, Bryn Mawr, and many other places, and they treated Edward as a fellow scholar in telling of their findings and their goals. Edward declined, however, to send his rarities away from his library, and he refused (for example) to mail the original manuscript of Thoreau's *Walden* to a scholar in Chicago. He was glad to provide photocopies, however, and he and his staff answered hundreds of inquiries from scholars everywhere, like those preparing a census of all Shakespeare quartos, a descriptive bibliography of fifteenth-century printed books, and a record of books printed in England before 1640. Many friends and fellow book lovers came to see his collection, and Edward enjoyed showing things of special interest to them. If he had recently acquired something he greatly enjoyed—which was most of the time—he took pleasure in reading passages from it to his visitors.

The fame of his library also spread in wider circles, and between 1915 and 1920 Edward came to be described as "The

Aerial view of the grounds in 1921, with the residence in the center and the Library above it and slightly to the right.

Prince of Book Collectors" and his collection as "the greatest private library in the world." He began to think about building a library on the ranch to house his collection. He hired Myron Hunt to visit libraries in the East with him, and they worked out plans together for a suitable structure. Construction took a little more than a year, and in 1920 the collection and staff moved from New York and began operations in their new home. Scholars were welcome, and they came in considerable numbers to carry out their own projects with the use of these rich resources.

In 1915 Edward had suffered a life-threatening illness of the prostate and bladder which incapacitated him for six months. For the rest of his life he had recurrent attacks of this ailment. Edward had to be catheterized twice a day, required regular physical therapy, and took a sleeping tablet nearly every night, much to the disapproval of his daughter Elizabeth. But his spirits remained good, and his natural optimism contributed to his constant pleasure in living. He was considered to be "a great kidder" by his valet and by the electrician who broke in his new shoes for him, and he was especially fond of jokes and funny stories and singing ditties while he was dressing in the morning.

In 1919 he took a crucially important step that he had been thinking about for almost twenty years, and it resulted in what was probably the greatest accomplishment of his life. He had long before said that he wanted "to give something to the public before he died" and that he regarded himself as "a trustee" of his books and manuscripts and art objects, with a responsibility for them "far greater" than that which attaches to the ownership of purely personal articles. So in 1919 he established a trust which became the Huntington Library, Art Collections, and Botanical Gardens. He gave to this trust all his books, manuscripts, and art objects, his library building, residence, and gardens, and ultimately $10 million in endowment funds. He retained a measure of control during his lifetime through the power to appoint the five trustees and to refine the definition of the trust's purposes within the general plan to advance learning in the arts and sciences and "to promote the public welfare" through the use of the library, the art gallery, and the gardens.

The public perception of Edward was gradually changing. In the first decade of the century he was chiefly valued as the individual who had done most for the development and growth of Southern California. Later he was valued for his moral qualities as a wise and far-sighted person. Finally he was seen as a benefactor to the public: as the one whose splendid gift would fundamentally influence the progress of the arts and letters in California and in the country as a whole. The spirit of idealism was strong in America at the time, and Edward fully shared it. There was an eagerness to believe that society could be essentially improved by the acts set in motion by one person, and praise was heaped on Edward for having given society "the most outstanding cultural endowment of modern times." In expressing his thanks for the appreciation offered him, Edward said, "I feel that the Library and Art Gallery will prove a means of pleasure and instruction to the people of California, and in the far future, as this wonderful country becomes more and more a factor in the growth of the Nation, I trust that this place of mine will play its part in the development of better men and women, and in this way, better citizens."

The acclaim that came to Edward was spontaneous, and people felt a sense of very personal gratitude to him. A modest man, he was always reluctant to allow himself to be publicized. Here, for example, is his answer to the Associated Press when they asked in 1918 for permission to do an article on his library: "Dear Sir: In answer to your letter of Sept. 5th, I would say that I do not care to have any articles at present about the Library. Yours truly, H. E. Huntington."

1920–1924

After the World War ended, Edward and Belle made two more trips to France (in 1920 and 1921) and stayed for about six months at the Chateau

Beauregard. Belle thoroughly enjoyed the life there, but because Edward was separated from his books and felt burdened by the overwhelming amount of decision making concerning the operation of the Chateau, he could not enjoy France. Finally, in 1921, Belle agreed with Edward to give up their lease on it.

The couple spent most of their time in New York. They lived a quiet, gracious, well-regulated life, as they had done ever since their marriage in 1913. Their entertaining was mainly for Archer (who had lunch with them nearly every day) and other family members. (Archer's wife Helen had left him in 1918 and gotten a divorce; in 1923 he married Anna Hyatt, the sculptor, and she joined the family circle.) They went to the theater occasionally and frequently spent a few days during the hot weather at their country place in Westchester County. Edward kept a business office downtown with a small staff where he went occasionally. His main activity, however, was dealing with his books—reading the old ones, becoming familiar with the new ones, and thinking about which would be the next ones. As he wrote to a friend, "I wish to get out of active business and fool away money on books and other things that give me pleasure."

The members of the Huntington family no longer went to Edward's childhood home in Oneonta. Edward bought out the interest of his siblings and in 1920 gave the house and adjacent property, along with some 10,000 books and an endowment of $200,000, to the city of Oneonta to provide a public library and park. The gift was a great success, and he was happy to have furnished his home town with "a means of recreation and improvement for both mind and body."

In the eleven years of their marriage, Edward and Belle spent just a little more than a third of their time in California. Edward thought the ranch was "the greatest place on earth" and "the only place in the world to live." He would have been glad to have stayed there all the time. But Belle did not like California and went there only to please Edward. She said she disliked the heat, but probably the real reason was that Archer was not there. She and Edward invited Archer regularly, and built a guest house for him, but he

Huntington with the ducks on the grounds (*above*), and holding a grandchild (*below*).

never came. Edward respected Belle's wishes and willingly lived where she wanted to be.

When they were in Southern California, Edward enjoyed himself thoroughly. He took long walks by himself through the grounds nearly every day to see the progress of the planting and to guide new developments. He visited the aviary and talked with the birds, played croquet with the grandchildren, sat on the loggia and read while enjoying the view, and spent the afternoons in the library with his books. Edward and Belle took occasional day trips in the area—to Santa Monica to have lunch with a friend, or to Mount Lowe or Long Beach—but would be safely home in San Marino by six o'clock, in time to dress for dinner. There was much sociability for Edward and Belle with family and guests at lunch and dinner. After dinner they would play cards whenever card-playing guests were there; auction bridge and hearts were the favorite games, and the evening entertainment ended around ten.

Belle could not walk very far and she enjoyed the house. She had a small dog and a green parrot (both named Buster) that she liked very much. The parrot could imitate Belle's voice so well that everyone mistook it for hers. One of Buster's favorite evening messages, when the parrot was upstairs and the family downstairs, was, "Edward, Edward, hurry up! Come up here! Go to bed!" Edward laughed heartily and thought it a great joke.

Edward occupied a suite on the southeast corner of the house on the second floor; it included the present corner room with a view over the San Gabriel Valley to the south and of the foothills and Mount Baldy to the east (the room that is now used for "conversation" paintings), and the adjacent rooms toward the west overlooking the valley. Homer Ferguson, the head of the Newport News Shipbuilding and Drydock Company, said that he was given a nearby room on his frequent visits because Edward liked to hear him sing in the shower. Belle's suite was adjacent to the corner room, on the east side of the house (later converted into a period room called the Quinn Room), which she and her companion occupied.

They had frequent house guests, and company nearly every day for lunch or dinner or both. Mostly they were Edward's relatives—his sister and his children (with their spouses and children) and his cousins—or his close local friends like the Pattons and the Dunns, or dealers who had become friends, like Joseph Duveen and A. S. W. Rosenbach.

Edward and Belle maintained a good deal of formality in their domestic life. When they were together, they always had a valet or a butler with them, or at least in the next room with the door open between them. "We have no secrets," she said. Whether they had guests or not, they dressed for dinner (black tie and long dress), and their dress was quite formal for all occasions. She wore handsome outfits and was always well groomed. Edward's valet said that she "always dressed like a queen" in long dresses that looked like wedding gowns, but in black versions after Collis's death in 1900; "she was so beautiful as she came down the stairway and walked down that long hall into the dining room." Edward dressed conservatively, mostly in gray, but Belle set a higher standard for him in favor of new clothes. Edward's argument that "your old shoes and your old clothes are your best friends" would not pass muster with her, and she insisted that all his clothes be new. She was the boss in all domestic details, and he did not object.

Belle did not like to have people who were not personal friends come on business or to see the pictures. Once when three business associates called on Edward in the evening, and stayed till quarter of eleven, she sent Edward's valet downstairs to "tell Mr. Huntington that I want him to go to bed and tell those three gentlemen that I said for them to go home." Within one minute, they left.

Edward and Belle both had many friends in Southern California. Leslie (Howard's wife), who came to have lunch with Belle whenever Belle was free, thought that Belle was "very alert and always capable of entertaining and meeting people most graciously under all conditions and at all times." All of Belle's friends thought that her mind was very bright and lively and strong, that she was keenly interested in what was going on around her, and that she was responsive to other people.

Edward had several close friends (like his attorney Billy Dunn and his neighbor George Patton), and they all admired the quickness

Huntington, at a baseball game with Los Angeles Railway employees, is in the center wearing a straw hat. Howard (in a bowler) is next to him.

of his mind in grasping the essence of a problem, his cordial friendliness, and his love of fun. He enjoyed the coupon-cutting contests that he and Dunn had whenever interest was due on his bonds. Each would start with a stack of fifty street-railway bonds and then cut the due coupon from each bond in his stack vying to see who would finish his stack first. The contest went on amid much laughter and merriment, but at the conclusion both the bonds and the coupons were returned to the vault, because the company could not afford to pay the interest due and still keep the five-cent fare. And Edward preferred to keep the five-cent fare. He was friendly and cordial toward all who worked for him. He always shook hands with the workmen and asked about them and their families. They felt free to talk with him about anything, and they sensed the genuineness of his personal interest in them, their families, and their well being.

No matter where he was, Edward kept acquiring books and art objects. In the five years before 1920, his art collection had almost doubled in its book value, to $7 million, with the purchase of paintings, tapestries, bronzes, furniture, and sculpture. But it was during the period 1920 to 1924 that he acquired such popular favorites as Gainsborough's *Blue Boy* and *The Cottage Door* and Reynolds's *Sarah Siddons as the Tragic Muse.* For twenty years Edward had admired and owned reproductions of the *Blue Boy*—which was often paired in the press with Leonardo's *Mona Lisa* as one of the pictures that had received more acclaim than any others in the world. When Duveen was able to get the two Gainsboroughs and the Reynolds from the Duke of Westminster for Edward, the public reaction was sensational. One hundred thousand people came to a special showing of *Blue Boy* in the National Gallery in London and mourned its departure, and an exhibition in New York brought out another large crowd to pay reverential homage to the painting. At last *Blue Boy* arrived in San Marino, and Edward declared that it was the painting "I take the greatest delight in" and hoped it would be "as great an attraction to future generations here." In these years Edward had purchased seventeen important British paintings at a total cost of $3.5 million.

Gainsborough's *Blue Boy* was acquired by Huntington in 1921.

Edward was also acquiring many books and manuscripts. He was always stepping into book shops to pick up things he wanted, reading catalogs, and buying entire collections when he could. Between 1920 and 1924 he bought forty-seven collections of substantial importance, comprising some 300,000 books and manuscripts. Edward was turning away from emphasis on expensive display items and moving toward material of scholarly value, like 66 royal charters before the year 1245, or 2,410 fifteenth-century printed books, or 40 Indian treaties, or 3,000 prime Lincoln items, or 12,000 early Washington items. Edward was by nature a specialist, and in these years he was making his collection into a scholar's library for the advancement of learning. Scholars used the library more and more after it was moved to California, libraries asked for photographs of material to fill their gaps, and the staff was kept busy answering the endless inquiries from scholars and libraries in England and the United States.

Early in 1923 Edward decided it would be a good idea to have portraits of Belle and himself painted. At first Belle was opposed because she thought herself "too old to be painted again," but at last she agreed. At Edward's request for advice, Duveen suggested the English painter Oswald Birley, and Archer concurred. Birley came to San Marino in the winter of 1923, and the sittings were held in the drawing room. He painted Edward first, in six sittings, and both Edward and Belle were pleased with the final result. Belle did not approve of his first sketch of her face because, she said, "you took my wrinkles away, you have made me young." She insisted that he start over and paint her "exactly as she was." He did so, and she liked the result.

Edward had to face a good many problems during these years, even when they were living in his chosen Southern California. He continued to suffer from frequent illnesses—colds that hung on, the flu, recurrences of his bladder and prostate problems. His daughters felt that he was losing more of his mental powers than natural aging would account for. As a preeminent public figure, Edward had to deal with an avalanche of letters and requests

Oswald Birley's portrait (1924) of Huntington.

and appeals; he tried to handle each of them thoughtfully (with the help of one secretary), and he found the task very burdensome. There were management problems with his business enterprises, which he had expected to operate successfully under his earlier policies with such occasional guidance as he chose to give without much delegation of authority. His businesses were in fact operating on the edge of failure because of their high debt ratio, and he refused to supply the cash they needed by any retrenchment or by issuance of bonds on his other properties. His managers appealed to him constantly for operating funds, and he always returned the

Oswald Birley's portrait (1924) of Arabella.

problem to them for solution. They found dealing with Belle even more difficult because her habit was to ignore bills and problems. There were similar difficulties in the Library, because Edward neither delegated authority nor provided active leadership. The trustees grumbled about their dissatisfaction, and there were tensions within the library staff. In 1924 George Watson Cole was eased out as librarian and replaced by Chester Cate; this change had lasted less than a year, when Cate committed suicide.

Edward's life was diminished during these years by the devastating deaths of a number of relatives and close associates. Three that struck him especially hard were the deaths of Epes Randolph (who had been a very close business associate and friend since the 1870s), his only son Howard (whose death from cancer devastated him), and Billy Dunn (whose death deprived him of his closest and dearest friend).

1924–1927

ut the most distressing event of all was the death of Belle in September 1924 in New York. Both had assumed, in the light of their medical histories, that she would survive him. But late in 1923 she became seriously ill in San Marino. Six months later, when they were ready to leave for New York, she had premonitions of her death; she told her ladies' luncheon group that "my time has come and my next trip to California will be in a box"; when Archer met Edward and Belle at the station in New York, Belle said, "Archer, you will never have to be at the depot again to meet your mother. This is my last trip." She died of pneumonia about three months later, after many blood transfusions and an operation on an abscessed kidney. Edward and Archer were constantly at her bedside during her last illness and at her death, and Edward reported that "in her delirium" she kept saying, "Take care of Edward."

Edward stayed in seclusion in the New York house for several weeks trying to regain his composure. He wrote to many friends about Belle's "goodness and kindness," and he found comfort in retiring to his library and reading his books. He and Archer were co-executors of her estate, which had a value of about $17 million after taxes. Almost all of it went to Archer, a small fraction went to institutions of prime interest to Archer and Collis, and there were some gifts to Belle's brothers' families and other relatives, but nothing to Edward or his children or his institution.

When Edward returned to San Marino in November 1924, he looked forward to staying there for the rest of his life. He gave up his New York offices and all his memberships in the East except for two book clubs, and he focused his full attention on the beauties of his ranch and on his institution. Much of the time his house was full of guests, mostly family, with a lot of people for meals. Belle's chair was always at the table, but no one was seated at her place. "I want to feel that Mrs. Huntington is alive," he told his valet. The house was attractive, and Edward enjoyed it along with his guests. The whole residence was full of paintings, but Edward's special favorites at this time were said to be *Sarah Siddons as the Tragic Muse* (in the main hall, seen immediately after entering the house), *Master William Blair* and *Lady Hamilton* in the south front hall, and *Blue Boy* and *Pinkie* side by side in the large drawing room. (The Main Gallery, where most of these paintings now hang, was added some years after Edward's death.) Edward usually saluted the *Blue Boy* when he left home and gave him a formal greeting upon his return.

Among the various notable visitors were Mr. and Mrs. John D. Rockefeller, Jr., and their three younger sons (David, Winthrop, and Laurance), who came for lunch and a day of visiting the Library, the residence, and the gardens. Edward was glad to get to know them better. Rockefeller, he noted with approval "takes quite seriously, as he should, the training of his children, and the three boys that were here were good types of American youths, and are being brought up in a most democratic way." Edward enjoyed a royal visit of two nights from the Swedish Crown Prince Gustavus Adolphus and Princess Louise, and he took pleasure in showing them books and manuscripts of special interest. At the formal dinner in their honor, his sister Carrie acted as hostess.

Edward's joy in Southern California was interrupted in the autumn of 1925 by the need to be hospitalized in Philadelphia because of a recurrence of his old prostate and bladder problem. During his stay in the hospital he was allowed to have visitors. On one occasion two close friends came at the same time: the book dealer Dr. Rosenbach sat on one side of his bed and the art dealer Sir Joseph Duveen on the other side. Edward, lying flat on his back with his arms outstretched, asked them if he reminded them of anyone. They were both nonplussed and had no answer. "Well, gentlemen," said Huntington jestingly, "I remind myself of Jesus Christ on the cross between the two thieves." Rosenbach and Duveen smiled weakly. After four days of examinations, Edward's prostate gland was surgically removed. (No mention was made of cancer, which by then had presumably spread beyond the prostate.) Within a few weeks he was able to go home, and he soon began to resume as active a life as he could. The operation was declared successful, but the incision never healed entirely and kept opening underneath the dressing.

As soon as he could, Edward walked across to the Library every day. He pushed the acquisitions program vigorously, and during the years 1925 to 1927 he made twenty-nine en bloc purchases of extensive collections of material on such topics as early British history, the American Revolution, women's suffrage, and Jack London, as he continued to develop a deeply representative collection of Anglo-American culture with materials that (as be said) "truly reflect the humanity of the times in which they were written."

He also bought ten major paintings during these years, including Constable's *View on the Stour near Dedham,* Gainsborough's *Karl Friedrich Abel,* and Lawrence's *Pinkie.* Edward was a little embarrassed at the amount of money he was spending for paintings ($380,000 for *Pinkie,* for example). "I cannot let the trustees know I have spent so much money," he confided to a friend. "They would raise an awful row if they knew." (At this time the trustees were trying to get Edward to devote his money to increasing the endowment.) Another art project that had been in Edward's mind ever since Belle's death was the establishment of a special art collection in the west wing of the Library in her memory. Archer agreed to give him the Birley portrait of Belle and the nineteen Italian primitives of which she had been particularly fond that had hung in the hall of the New York house. Edward bought a great many other things—furniture, clocks, porcelain, and sculpture—at a cost of about $2 million to complete the memorial. He was very happy to report to Archer the high opinion of a few intimate friends who had seen it "that it is quite worthy, in its beauty, of the lovely character which we both loved."

The planning for the mausoleum was another act of loving remembrance by Edward for Belle. She had chosen the site, during one of their evening strolls, on a hillock just north of their residence. "Don't you think this would be a nice place to be buried?" she asked him. "Edward, I would like to be buried here, right here where I have my shoes." He agreed. When the time came to design a mausoleum, he decided that a round marble structure in the form of a Greek temple would be best and, after looking at many pictures and sketches, he engaged the architect John Russell Pope to realize the design. Edward was delighted with the plan and with the model, which he thought "a great work of art. I have never seen anything in modern architecture which appeals to me more than this does," he said. He visited the site frequently to watch the construction. Once, after the sar-

The mausoleum, erected by Huntington on the site chosen by Arabella.

cophagus was in place, he pushed up against it with his cane and said playfully to the contractor, "I guess this will hold me all right." The mausoleum was not completed until after Edward's death. The architect then used it as the prototype for his design of the Jefferson Memorial in Washington, D. C.

Edward made some important refinements to the stated objectives of his institution during these years. In the original trust indenture, it was described as a library, art gallery, museum, and park, intended "to promote the public welfare." In 1925 and 1926, it was more specifically defined as a research institution of educational value to the public, and provision was made for a director, research associates, and fellows. Simultaneously, Edward wanted it to serve a broader public. Belle had always objected to admitting the public to the grounds, the Library, and the residence, and he had respected her wishes. After her death, outside groups were allowed in, and on March 18, 1925, the institution was officially opened to the general public on a limited basis. Many choice rare books and manuscripts were put on special display in the Library. According to the librarian, Edward "stood out on the lawn and watched the people attending the exhibit. He seemed very pleased." The next day he said, "My purpose in creating this foundation was to make it for the benefit of the world. It is for all people who may find use for it." He was happy that "many students, writers and authorities on historical and literary matters" were already using it, and now he could take pleasure in seeing the general public share in the enjoyment of his gift.

In the spring of 1927, Edward's doctor insisted that he return to Philadelphia for further surgery, since the incision would not heal. He went cheerfully and optimistically, in the expectation of returning home after two or three weeks. In the hospital, the last book he read was a recent account of the Lincoln-Douglas debate in Peoria in 1854 by a man who had attended it as a child. The last book he looked at before the operation, however, was the *Short-Title Catalogue* of English books of the period 1475 to 1640—an area in which his own collection was outstanding.

The operation was regarded as successful, though Edward found it very painful. His family was at the hospital with him. He grew progressively weaker; presumably the cancer had spread through his body beyond the capabilities of surgery to remove it. He died on the morning of May 23, 1927. His last known words were a call for Belle. At the end he sighed, smiled faintly, and closed his eyes. That afternoon all flags were flown at half mast on the buildings of the City and County of Los Angeles and of the City of Pasadena.

The casket containing Edward's remains was conveyed to his house in his private railroad car. It was met in San Marino by the local troop of Boy Scouts and by the staff of the Library and Botanical Gardens. A simple funeral service was held in the library room of the residence, with Belle's portrait placed near the casket; the casket was then taken to the grave site, placed next to Belle's, and the two were covered with freshly cut flowers. The minister read a short passage from the *Pilgrims' Progress* and offered one final, brief prayer.

At the time of Edward's death, there were many thoughtful appraisals of his accomplishments, and it may be instructive to recall what it was about him that most struck his contemporaries. First, he was universally regarded as the preeminent American book collector. Second, he was honored as a model American because he amassed a great fortune by hard, intelligent work and then devoted it to the betterment of those who were to come after him. Third, he was perceived as a quiet, open, friendly person of deep modesty and kindness. It was in ways like these that people of his own time thought about him.

Since Edward's death, his accomplishments as a collector of books and art have come to seem even more awesome than they appeared to his contemporaries, and his public-spirited contribution to American education and culture has been appreciated by hundreds of scholars and millions of visitors. Though the generations that have followed him cannot know the private and unassuming Edward personally, his tastes and character are immortalized in his legacy of gardens, pictures, and books.

FURTHER READING

Bernal, Peggy Park. ***The Huntington Library, Art Collections, and Botanical Gardens.*** San Marino: Huntington Library, 1992.

Dickinson, Donald C. ***Henry E. Huntington's Library of Libraries.*** San Marino: Huntington Library, 1995.

Hertrich, William. ***The Huntington Botanical Gardens, 1905–1949: Personal Recollections of William Hertrich.*** San Marino: Huntington Library, 1988.

Thorpe, James. ***Henry Edwards Huntington: A Biography.*** Berkelely: The University of California Press, 1994.

Wilson, Diana. ***The Mausoleum of Henry and Arabella Huntington.*** San Marino: Huntington Library, 1989.

The Huntington Art Collections: A Handbook. San Marino: Huntington Library, 1986.

BOOKS-IN-PRINT CATALOG

HUNTINGTON LIBRARY PRESS
1151 Oxford Road, San Marino, CA 91108
Phone 818·405·2172   Fax 818·585·0794